MANXIETY

PROVOCATIONS

MANXIETY

THE DIFFICULTIES OF BEING MALE

DYLAN JONES

SERIES EDITOR:
YASMIN ALIBHAI-BROWN

Biteback Publishing

First published in Great Britain in 2016 by
Biteback Publishing Ltd
Westminster Tower
3 Albert Embankment
London SE1 7SP
Copyright © Dylan Jones 2016

ISBN 978-1-78590-082-2

10 9 8 7 6 5 4 3 2 1

A CIP catalogue record for this book is available from the British Library.

Set in Stempel Garamond by Adrian McLaughlin

Printed and bound in Great Britain by
CPI Group (UK) Ltd, Croydon CR0 4YY

Contents

Introduction and acknowledgements

'Not all men are annoying.
Some are dead…'

– PINTEREST GREETING CARD

A FEMALE FRIEND OF mine was speaking at a conference in Oxford recently. The subject was women and power (I think she gets asked to talk at a lot of things like this). On her return to London, she said she was feeling enervated and beleaguered.

'For five hours', she said, 'the speakers went on and on about female rights and the problems with men.'

Two cameramen were there throughout the day and I asked one of them how he felt. He simply said, 'I wish someone had said something about what men are going through too, or just said something nice about those of us who are actually trying. My brother killed himself last year and it was because he was so full of self-doubt about whether he could be good enough for a woman. He had also just been sacked by a new boss who happened to be female – and this was after eight years working for his employer. Does he not matter?'

Suicide rates for young men in the UK are tragically high; it is now the biggest killer of men under the age of forty-five, and in 2014 twelve men died by their own hand every single day. Feminism has obviously changed the world for the better in so many ways, but it has also left many men feeling lost and dislocated. University and school results show that men are failing badly. My friend said that, in her opinion, feminism has become complacent, and it's certainly easy to see how some of its more extreme practitioners seem unconcerned about both the physical and emotional pressures on men these days – what have become known as 'manxieties'.

They ought to be concerned. Anxiety disorders among men are no longer treated with suspicion by doctors, a situation helped enormously by the number of bold-face names who have admitted to having some sort of depression, including Johnny Depp, John Cleese, Stephen Fry, Mickey Rourke, Jim Carrey and, tragically, Robin Williams. They have drawn attention to the fact that a lot of men these days feel unable to cope – with work, with partners, peers, family, with the undue pressures of the modern world.

So, could it be time for a men's movement? Something that encourages men to 'fight back'? Something to bring them back into the fold?

In this short book we shall take a look, and then take a view. My friend was of course Yasmin Alibhai-Brown, who suggested there might be something in all of this. I thought so too, although I think we may have reached slightly different conclusions (she appears more inclined to go in to bat for the men than I do). So I'd like to thank her, as well as Iain Dale, Sir Alex Ferguson, Ed Victor, and the women in my family (who I don't think are prepared to go in to bat for me, either).

Part I

British men today: backward, in crisis, or evolving?

'Men are like fine wine – they all start out like grapes, and it's our job to stomp on them and keep them in the dark until they mature into something we'd like to have dinner with.'

– ANONYMOUS

AT THE TAIL end of 2015, a YouGov poll for *Prospect* magazine suggested that white men in their twenties have become the most derided social group in Britain. According to the poll, there is an general expectation among British people that young, white men are lazy and rude, spend their time getting drunk and are more likely to have several sexual partners at one time. They are also the demographic group least likely to go to university.

It cannot be denied that the enormous social changes in the last half a century have profoundly undermined the cultural identity, community cohesion and solidarities of male, white, working-class lives. Apprenticeships have all but gone, close-knit, working-class communities have been shattered by the eradication of local industries, and with them a certain amount of pride and self-respect. Role models these days are in seriously short supply. Commenting on the poll, Mike Savage in *The Observer* wrote:

> [Once] there was a strong sense of male pride and self-respect, often exemplified in loyal membership of trade unions. And a degree of respect was also accorded more generally to the 'hardy souls of toil'. Coalminers, engine

4

drivers, shipbuilders and the like had a heroic resonance that was recognised – sometimes grudgingly – throughout British society. This was a world in which young white men could feel self-respect and a sense that they were subordinate to no one…

Over the last fifty years this world has collapsed. Swaths of deindustrialisation have removed vast areas of skilled manual work, with their attendant cultures of respectability and autonomy, leaving young men having to navigate a casual and insecure labour market.

And to find their way in a world that doesn't appear to afford them much respect. Football has been appropriated by the middle classes (what former Manchester United captain Roy Keane once called 'the prawn sandwich brigade'), pubs have been gentrified beyond belief and boxing has all but been outlawed; while the very idea of a respectable working class has been replaced by the fear of a Neanderthal underclass. Even the 'lad' became gentrified in the 1990s, being traduced and stylised in the same breath, being both celebrated and lampooned in magazines such as *Loaded*, *Maxim* and *FHM*. Men were fed a diet of *Men Behaving Badly*, while their younger brothers were encouraged to lap up *The Inbetweeners*. Lad culture was defined as a marketable term, but it only took a few years before the very idea of being a lad became reductive, and he ended up, ten years later, in a worse place than where he started: mocked by a liberal media elite who didn't want any more sloppily dressed oiks at the party.

Dr Mary Curnock Cook, the chief executive of university admissions service UCAS, said recently that 'with further increases in the gap between men and women entering higher education, we can now see clearly that concentrating outreach efforts on young men, particularly white men, would make a significant contribution to diminishing the rich–poor gap'.

It seems all of us are intimidated by women these days, whether we're rich or poor, black or white. According to new research, despite claiming to find intelligent women attractive, men choose not to date someone who is smarter than themselves. We feel threatened by intelligent women and, according to the study, we state our theoretical preference for smart women only to then change our minds before committing to a date. Psychologists at the University at Buffalo, California Lutheran University and University of Texas at Austin asked 105 men to rank the merits of women who had out- or underperformed them in an intelligence test as a prospective partner. They found that the men were more likely to declare their attraction to women who had performed better than them. 'Men formed favourable impressions and showed greater interest in women who displayed more (versus less) intelligence than themselves,' the study authors wrote. However, 'men who had been told they were about to meet a more intelligent woman distanced themselves more from her, tended to rate her as less attractive, and showed less desire to exchange contact information or plan a date with her'. 'Feelings of diminished masculinity accounted for men's decreased attraction toward women who outperformed them,' the report concluded.

As the *Medical Daily* website said at the time, 'For men, apparently, having an intelligent girlfriend is like having a pet wolf – cool in theory, but not something you'd want in real life.'

Manxiety

These days you find this time and time again, as men feel slighted by the people they work for (or don't), by the friends they feel they can't possibly compete with, by the ungrateful children they have spawned, and by the women they date. Masculinity, it seems, is in crisis, as more and more men claim to be suffering from 'manxiety' (the problems associated with being labelled as a 'man' and all that it implies) and feelings of inadequacy and fearlessness. It seems not a week goes by when men are not being accused of being too violent, too stupid or too sexual. The MP Diane Abbott ranted about 'hypersexuality' at a DEMOS lecture not so long ago, berating men for being sexually aggressive in the city, on our streets and on campuses. In her eyes, hypersexuality is 'a celebration of heartlessness with a lack of respect for women's autonomy'.

She isn't the only one who thinks so – not by a long chalk – and it's freaking men out.

In 2014, encouraged by the success of their blog, Holly Baxter and Rhiannon Lucy Cosslett wrote a very angry (but extremely well-reviewed) book called *The Vagenda*, in which men's magazine consumers were all labelled 'lads' who aspired to a 'frat boy mentality' – 'a delicious combo of sport, heavy drinking and dehumanising attitudes to women propagated by close-knit groups of all-male "homosocial" [good word] bell-ends with whom you'd never want to share a tent at a festival'. I don't know anyone who'd want to share a tent with people like this either, especially at a music festival, but the inference is clear: men are dweebs, and if you're not, prove it. No one in the media, it seems, is innocent:

the *Daily Telegraph* of all things is referred to as 'a newspaper so scarily feminist it has its own "men" section'.

But then we know that women say bad things about men. The thing is, it's no longer women telling men how appalling they are nowadays; it's men doing it too. Diminished by feminists, mocked by their peers and ridiculed by the media, all our self-esteem has evaporated, vanished into nothing.

Last year, the internationally acclaimed psychologist Philip Zimbardo and his research partner Nikita D. Coulombe blamed it all on technology. In *Man (Dis)connected* they argued that digital technologies create alternative realities that many men find less demanding and more rewarding than real life. They suggested that because of this, our evaluations of sex and relationships are stunted, making it difficult for us to socialise and connect with anyone who isn't encased in a mobile phone or a tablet. Obsessively watching pornography makes us sociopathic, while compulsively gaming turns us into addicts.

'There are a record number of young men who are flaming out academically, wiping out socially with girls, and failing sexually with women,' they write.

> You don't have to look too far to see what we're talking about; everyone knows a young man who is struggling. Maybe he's under-motivated in school, has emotional disturbances, doesn't get along with others, has few real friends or no female friends, or is in a gang. He may even be in prison. Maybe he's your son or relative. Maybe he's you.

These days, men just don't feel comfortable acting on impulse or behaving recklessly. According to a Scottish university study, compared with the action men of the 1970s and 1980s, today's men are wimps – far less interested in adrenalin-junkie pastimes such as parachuting, scuba diving and mountaineering than the previous generation. The School of Psychology and Neuroscience at the University of St Andrews found men's willingness to engage in physically challenging activities has tailed off dramatically in the past forty years, since the tests were first carried out. Dr Kate Cross, who led the academic team, says that 'the decline could reflect declines in average fitness levels, which might have reduced many people's interest in physically challenging activities. Alternatively, the questions were designed in the 1970s so they could now be out of date. Skiing, for example, may no longer be viewed as a novel or intense activity.' She also says that the rise of the computer generation in the intervening years – coupled, perhaps, with increasing attention to health and safety – may have taken the edge off a thirst for adventure. All in all, men are becoming far more nervous about taking risks.

In 2012, Hanna Rosin wrote *The End of Men: And the Rise of Women*, a book that catalogued this phenomenon. 'This is an astonishing time,' read the blurb. 'In a job market that favours people skills and intelligence, women's adaptability and flexibility make them better suited to the modern world.' The stats bore this out: women in Britain hold down half the jobs; women own over 40 per cent of China's private businesses; in 1970 women in the US contributed to 2–6 per cent of the family income, while now it is 42.2 per cent. Rosin focused on the 'mancession' or 'he-cession' that had hit American men hard, ill-preparing them for the post-manufacturing, post-industrial age. These jobless, career-less men had to make do with the trinkets of 'ornamental masculinity', as the critic Susan Faludi once called it – all the macho accessories and Hollywood superheroes that are now the staple diet of the disenfranchised male.

'Men today, especially young men, are in a transition moment,' she says.

They no longer want to live as their fathers did, marrying women they can't talk to, working long hours day after day, coming home to pat their kids on the head absentmindedly. They understand that the paternal white boss, like the one on *The Office*, has now become a punch line. But they can't turn away from all that because they fear how power and influence could be funnelled away from them; by wives who earn more money than they do, jobs with less prestige, tedious Tuesday afternoons at the playground. There are plenty of opportunities for men. Theoretically, they can be anything these days: secretary, seamstress, PTA president. But moving into new roles, and a new phase, requires certain traits: flexibility, hustle, and an expansive sense of identity.

Which, according to both men and women alike, we simply don't have.

The new minority

We certainly shy away from traditional forms of identification. In days gone by, being male, middle-class, and middle-aged was considered to be a sign of success in Britain, almost a badge of honour. You could be failing at your job, unlucky in love and disconnected from your family, but you could still hold your head up in the golf club and the saloon bar because you were a man with a Jag parked outside your house.

Not anymore, though – and not for some time.

A few years ago, in February 2008 in fact, the Radio 4 *Woman's Hour* presenter Jane Garvey said her programme was 'too middle-class', as though this were an inherently bad thing. She didn't endear herself to her listeners by saying her programme focused too much on cooking and women's problems and should probably be more upbeat to attract younger listeners, but the main thrust of her interview with *The Guardian*, or at least the thing she said that resonated the most, was the middle-classness of it.

> One of my bugbears about it would be – and they know this – that there is too much about the negative side of being female and not enough about the many good factors … I would also like to have less middle-class

ladies talking about cookery. Although there is nothing wrong with cookery … I think there is a massively middle-class bent to every programme on Radio 4. Find me a programme that isn't like that.

There are few things that could be more British than the middle class, but they are an endangered species, especially the men. Don't believe me? Just look around you. And ask men if they're happy being labelled that way. They hate it, find it emasculating, whereas women never think of it at all. Men either want to be oiks or toffs, not the chap in the middle. The middle classes are the new minority.

Many years ago, as the 1970s swiftly turned into the 1980s, I was briefly a member of a post-punk group called the Timing Association, an overly intense, art-school five-piece whose songs weren't quite as clever as Orange Juice and not quite as loud as Buzzcocks.

Having released a single – 'It's Magic' (and you won't be surprised to learn that it wasn't, not in the slightest, not at all) – we began having 'creative differences', argu-ing on a daily basis about everything from the singer's hair (the rest of us thought it was too short), to the lead guitarist's trousers (too wide, made of denim, wrong provenance). The only thing we could agree on was our name: it was rubbish.

But what did it for us, the thing that caused us to split up before our 'ground-breaking eponymous first album' (our first single was our final single) was class. One night, after a torturous rehearsal in the middle of Leyton in north London (the band practising next door was called the Armitage Shanks Band), our singer, Colin (you can tell we weren't going to be big), promp-tly walked out, throwing his metaphorical toys out of the pram as he often did.

'What's wrong?' I asked as he pushed open the heavy studio door.

'I can't work with him [the lead guitarist] anymore,' he said, looking for all the world like a man who had just been asked if he had ever slept with his sister.

'Why not?' I countered, feeling a little like Bette Davis in some 1930s melodrama.

'Why not?!' he screamed in his broken Midlands drawl. 'He's middle-class, that's why not. And I can't play in a band with someone who's middle-class.'

I was only nineteen at the time, and I'd rarely heard that most fundamental of British diseases articulated with such clarity. The ability to claim a working-class background was all the rage at the time, and, as being one of the defining tenets of punk rock, one that most of us involved felt duty-bound to lie about. The divisions between the middle class and the working class (who had only recently stopped being labelled 'lower class') were never more pronounced – at least not for my generation – and musicians and journalists alike would bang on for ages in the music press about 'authenticity', and how any kind of privileged background (i.e. not being brought up in a council flat in Hackney) was mutually exclusive to 'cool', 'credibility' and acceptability.

For the Timing Association, the clock had stopped,

although we almost felt at the vanguard of something when we heard that a short while later the Specials – who had just had an enormous hit with 'Ghost Town' – had essentially split up for the same reason, their singer Terry Hall complaining that it was difficult for him to work in a band that contained middle-class musicians (referring to the band's founder, Jerry Dammers).

Back in the heady days of punk, as soon as a band were discovered to be middle-class, and – worse – intent on disguising the fact, the critics started sharpening their pencils and oiling their Remingtons. There were precious few who escaped this forensic attention, and even fewer who were let off. Joe Strummer was one, strangely. The son of a diplomat (not the son of a bank robber) and educated at public school, when he joined the punk fraternity he totally changed the way he spoke, adopting an almost subterranean mockney drawl that only the Sex Pistols' John Lydon had the gumption to ever question. (Interviewer: 'Do you really hate Joe Strummer?' John Lydon: 'Of course not. Joe's a very nice bloke. He's just ashamed of his own class roots.') Mick Jagger, on the other hand, the most famous mockney of them all, didn't care what people thought of him, and his appropriation of someone else's voice was always thought of as either cute or faintly ridiculous; and because he wasn't aligned to any movement – or at least no movement celebrating the overthrow of a cultural orthodoxy by a largely proletarian underclass – he was welcomed as a harmless cartoon. Of course, the '60s were completely about class empowerment, but there was no 'year zero' like there was in the '70s, and you didn't have to disguise where you came from. And in Jagger's case, the voice didn't really kick in until later.

Class was important when we were young, and it was openly referred to in our house. My parents were part of a generation who had escaped the working class through sheer hard work, by devoting themselves to bettering themselves and embracing the social mobility of the 1950s and '60s. They were under the impression that being aspirational was a thoroughly decent thing, almost a *raison d'être*. Although they knew the path to prosperity wasn't smooth. 'Everyone will hate you when you grow up because you're middle-class,' my mother told me encouragingly when I was about fourteen.

> The upper classes will hate you because they'll think you're encroaching upon them; the working class will hate you because you're trying to leave them behind; and the middle class will hate you because they see themselves in you, and don't want to be reminded of where they came from. And they all came from the same place.

But that was long ago, before the death of our manufacturing industry and the birth of the leisure class, before Thatcherism made class a by-product of economic reform. If you were part of the economic miracle, you found your way into a gated community; if you weren't, you ended up on a sink estate. The working class became the underclass as everyone else supposedly became middle-class, seduced by the thought of a job in 'light industrial', a semi in a Home Counties new town and a spanking new burgundy Mondeo.

Of course, the middle classes are different to what they used to be, but they aren't fundamentally different. As Penny Wark said in *The Times* a while ago, 'What distinguishes the contemporary middle classes is that they have established new ways of identifying themselves. The affluent are middle-class because they have the money, the educated are middle-class irrespective of whether they have money, and we live among people like ourselves because that way we belong.'

It's instinctive as much as anything else, but why are we afraid of saying so? In particular, why are men afraid of saying so?

New Labour even tried to convince us we were living in a classless society, a meritocracy with no glass ceilings and no class barriers. 'We're all middle-class now,' the former Deputy Prime Minister John Prescott famously said in 1997, although you'd be hard-pushed to find anyone to admit to it these days. Under classifications produced by the Office for National Statistics, more than half the population is embraced by the new middle class. Over 50 per cent of us now fit the traditional middle-class classifications of A, B and C1 (those who work in professional, managerial and other white-collar jobs) for the first time in British history. The proportion working in manual jobs, what we used to call the working class, has fallen from 75 per cent a century ago, via 36 per cent in 1987, to 12 per cent today.

But try getting anyone to own up to it. We just don't want to know. Being middle-class has become anathema to the modern ideal, to the very idea of being modern. And where once the middle class were inviolate, now they are besieged at every turn.

And men suffer more than women. Just think of how many middle-class men drop their aitches; women never do.

A recent report from the National Centre for Social Research proved that, far from enjoying the fruits of upward social mobility, most people aspire to the bottom of the barrel, or at least enjoy giving the perception that they do. A staggering 57 per cent of Britons believe themselves to be working-class, ignoring the fact that only a relatively small percentage are actually employed in traditionally poorly paid, low-prestige jobs. Middle-class angst has manifested itself as a socio-economic diaspora, a nation of mockneys in Great Estuarial Britain. At the time, the *Daily Telegraph* did a vox pop of public figures, asking them which social class they considered themselves to belong to, and it was shocking how many middle-class notables found it impossible to admit to their ranking. Everyone had some sort of excuse, some clever way of denying their birthright: 'professional class', 'bohemian class', 'classless', 'the class of educated people', 'upper working class' – even 'business class', as though they'd simply been asked to choose how they'd like to fly. The new moneyed middle class, those who rise through the ranks, still think of themselves as well-to-do working-class; while the traditional middle class find themselves incapable of owning up to what they are: 'Well, I suppose you could call us middle-class, although we're not really like that at all.' Like what? Such is the stigma of being middle-class in the twenty-first century. Bizarrely, at an age when many men might reasonably be expected to join the establishment, I fear they are in danger of becoming a minority.

Even David Cameron has a problem with the classification. When I first interviewed him for *GQ* and asked him whether he was middle-class or upper-class he said, a little disingenuously, 'I don't really buy these labels.' When I pushed, he said, 'Gun to my head, I suppose I'd describe myself as well-off. I don't buy these class things because they're all going. What do these labels mean anymore?' Of course, he would never want to admit to being upper-class (which he most certainly is), but if he hates being called upper-class so much, what on earth is wrong with being called middle-class?

These days, being middle-class is as socially acceptable as herpes. In fact, I hear that in certain circles the latter is positively an advantage: 'Those with a sexually transmitted disease signifying a wayward and therefore socio-economically fashionable past to the left; those of you determined not to employ a glottal stop or aspire to drive a white van to the right.'

And boy, do they mean the right. Politically, the middle class is nowadays demonised as unacceptably right-wing, upholders of the sort of family values no longer aspired to by the new, meritocratic, working class, or the politically correct metropolitan commentariat. Where once the worst thing you could accuse the middle class of was aspiring to a petit bourgeois lifestyle, these days its members are assumed to be politically venal rather than politically apathetic.

It's worse, obviously, if you're a man.

When Paul Dacre, the editor-in-chief of the *Daily Mail* – the bastion of old-fashioned, male, middle-class values – spoke out against the tyranny of the British media's liberal agenda he was criticised by every left-wing journalist with access to a column. And what did Dacre espouse? Oh, simply madcap ideas like community, clamping down on crime, curtailing immigration, monitoring the welfare state and celebrating marriage.

'Now, more than ever, we need our middle classes,' he said. 'What possible explanation can there be [for fewer claiming to be middle-class these days]? Well, one immediately springs to mind. It is that under New Labour, the liberal chatterers who constitute so much of the media and established political class openly sneer at the middle classes.'

Not only that, but we – the middle class, for I am one of the few people to readily admit my class – are now penalised for being the engine of prosperity, for being educated and aspirant. School leavers are penalised by a university admission policy that encourages ethnicity above qualifications, we have been told that in future we could be taxed for having pleasant homes with attractive views, and road pricing – should it ever come in – will fall especially heavily on the middle classes. Though many middle-class inhabitants can't afford the property or the big-ticket items they may have aspired to a generation ago (their class being visible more in smaller consumer choices, particularly those concerning culture), their values and their aspirations for their children, and their obsessive devotion to educating them, is not only what sets them apart, it's what defines them. And yet they are castigated for this – even by other members of their class. Even the middle classes hate each other sometimes. According to *The Times*, 'The middle classes drink too much. They're in debt. They worry about their health. They agonise over their children's education and are prepared to tell porkies to get their kids into a good school.'

Culturally, 'middle-class' is now the ultimate pejorative, and belonging to the middle class – or at least admitting to being middle-class – is fast becoming as socially unacceptable as voting Tory still is to the Islington Media Mafia. In 1995, when she gave her infamous MacTaggart Lecture at the Edinburgh Television Festival, Janet Street-Porter challenged the 'male, middle-class, middle-aged' orthodoxy of TV executives as though the poor sods were rapists or muggers. In his BBC4 short film *The New Middle Classes*, broadcast in 2007, Tim Lott said that 'the children of Thatcher and Blair don't want to be middle-class, they just want more stuff. I call them the moregeoisie.' When critics accuse the middle class of being 'smug', it's implicit that they obviously don't think they're middle-class themselves. But, I ask myself, what exactly do they think they are?

Ironically – and how laden that word is with sarcasm – being labelled middle-class assumes that you have for some reason 'had it easy', as though it is only the working class who can pull themselves up by their boot laces (or are allowed to), ignoring the middle classes' obsession with self-fulfilment, with betterment, with the work ethic. Forget not that members of the middle class – or at least what we think of as the middle class these days – are simply the offspring of the working class who made good, who had the opportunity, the luck and the determination to 'get on'. Despising the middle class is not snobbery, it's a refusal to acknowledge a thirst for success, as though wanting to be middle-class was somehow a demonstration of anti-socialist values.

This has nothing to do with the dignity of labour, has little to do with any identification with the working class of yore. No, for the new, culturally downwardly mobile generation, culture and individuality are more important than heritage or family. 'Nowadays, most of those who claim to be working-class had middle-class parents,' says the psychologist Oliver James. 'They aspire to working classness because of its associations with authenticity – and to conceal the proverbial silver spoon in their mouth.'

Where once the difference between the middle and the working class was a determination by the former to use the word 'loo' instead of 'toilet', nowadays the differences revolve around the latter's determination to wear outlandish designer clothes and talk like a mockney.

And men, obviously, are the worst offenders, because they are the ones everyone is staring at. Because, these days, men are more defined by class than ever before.

It seems everyone has got it in for us.

Devaluing masculinity

In the last twenty-five years or so, men have been traduced by everyone, including those people (presumably both male and female) responsible for the television schedules. A few years ago, the schedules in this country began being saturated with shows in which so-called experts rampaged through people's houses, exposing their appalling consumer decisions and lack of flair for interior design. Essentially this was the type of television that had no qualms about mocking the working class, one that television people openly referred to as 'watching the chavs' (television people can be like that). One of the worst examples was a programme called *DIY SOS* (a typical example of how tabloid television programmes in the 'oos were usually named after their production shorthand: for example, a show that had been conjured up in a hotel bar by some tipsy TV producers and then nicknamed 'Pregnant White Trash' would have ended up on-screen as a show called, er, 'Pregnant White Trash'), in which the dismal incompetence of married men was exposed and lampooned for all to see. The trick was to get their wives and girlfriends to call the show, like they may have called the Ghostbusters, asking for expert help. It may have been funny on paper, but – turning the notion on its head – can you really imagine a show in which men, dissatisfied with their wives' ironing or washing-up skills, called in the BBC for help? Secondly, as one critic said at the time, 'Consider the premise of the show: men should be able to do DIY and women shouldn't. If men can't, women don't learn to do it them-selves, they go whining to a higher authority.'

'Contemporary advertising reflects a world where women hold the whip hand,' said Tony Parsons at the time. 'The reason is not just the supremacy of female purchasing power ... today's advertising reflects a world where women have cultural dominance. A world gone female.'

Parsons is a polemicist, a man who can distil an argument in the finest tabloid form, and therefore always gets to the nub of the problem. 'Why do you think this country hasn't been invaded for 1,000 years? Because Sporty Spice has an impressive collection of tattoos? Because of men.'

Even the world of design has followed suit, rounding the edges of masculine symbolism and pumping out a succession of bubble-gum coloured, ergonomic, soft-shell, curly-whirly designs that are meant to appeal not just to women, but also to men's feminine side. Cars, sanding machines, laptops, shovels, sideboards, cooking knives – everything these days is produced with an eye on the female customer. After all, women have more money than they've ever had, more than men in some sectors, and they don't need men to tend for them or spend for them.

One can also shoot a menacing glance at Richard Curtis, for creating a klutz archetype that has almost become a male role model. In both *Four Weddings and a Funeral* and *Notting Hill*, Hugh Grant played a feminised, tongue-tied wimp rescued from an apparently permanent state of sexual indecision by a strong, decisive Alpha Woman – Andie MacDowell in the first; Julia Roberts in the second. Not only does Curtis paint Grant as a hopeless fool who can only be redeemed by strident women, but the fact that Grant was a tremendously good-looking romantic hero meant that his stereotype quickly became accepted as a female ideal. Boys, you can only get the girl if you act like a dweeb (a good-looking dweeb, natch). Or by feigning femininity.

Where once we were cavemen, encouraged by the advertising ideal of the New Man, the previous two generations of men have become quiche men.

'Boys are bad, girls are good,' said the critic Bryan Appleyard when expounding on this topic.

Masculinity is an antisocial pathology and if, biologically, you must be a man, then you must also become an emotional transvestite. The death of Princess Diana endorsed the whole process. After that, caring was all that counted – the rest was just football hooliganism, villainous paparazzi, paedophiles and racists. There were no good men; the idea was a contradiction in terms.

Even self-proclaimed Hot Feminist Polly Vernon thinks men have become vaguely silly. In her book – subtitled *Modern Feminism With Style, Without Judgement* – she spends a whole chapter affectionately and entertainingly eulogising men, although you get the sense that she finds us vaguely preposterous.

I like it when they try and civilise themselves by acquiring one of the set of recently approved-for-use-by-men life skills, the kind of thing which might have seemed a tad effete a year or two ago, but is now terribly fashionable, to wit: 1) knowing something about cocktails, 2) attending a weekend residential course on learning how to bake your own sourdough bread, 3) ostentatiously growing out very specific areas of facial hair, 4) cycling while wearing head to toe Lycra, 5) making more dapper sock choices, 6) using emojis in text messages.

Vernon is playing for laughs, yet the humour is based in a reality that is echoed by women far less funny than Polly.

The subjugation of men has become a sport. In fact, it's almost an orthodoxy – a default position among women who see men solely as casual sex partners, occasional suppliers of sperm and the kind of people who can be relied upon to tell good jokes at parties.

The problem these days is that most of the good jokes are at men's expense.

'I have to pretend Matt earns more in front of certain of his friends, when really I earn, like, *much* more,' says one of her friends in her book.

And he's never asked me to do it, I just do; because I'm scared I'll emasculate him if I don't, but seriously: what the fuck? I emasculate ten men before lunchtime at work! I *like* emasculating men at work. It's what I do for fun! Why, then, do I go to such lengths to avoid emasculating this one specific man in a gastropub on Sundays?

We have become objects of pity.

In devaluing masculinity, we have lost far more than we thought, as political correctness and the absurdness of extreme feminism has all but eliminated the possibility of treating any male trait as a virtue.

The New Lads and the New Man

The immediate backlash to all this was Lad culture, but look where that got us. When the New Man emerged in the mid-1980s – a feminised man who did the shopping and dared to consume – he wasn't necessarily a feminist man, but he was definitely narcissistic. As the critic Jon Savage said at the time,

> The dominant New Man advert is remarkable indeed for its *absence* of women: women are either a threat (at their most extreme, personifying the Aids virus in *Fatal Attraction*) or simply irrelevant to the new, self-enclosed world of male pleasure and vanity. Far from marking a real change in gender roles, the New Man is yet another example of masculinity's privileged status in our society – the same old wolf in designer clothing.

Ouch. Well, if you thought he was bad, the New Lad was even worse (more about this later).

One of the things that men complain about today is their loss of identity, the fact that we don't have the same roles as we used to, and are therefore confused about where we stand in the world, at least compared to women. 'Society and requirements impose many expectations on us,' wrote the US relationship counsellor Jon Pease in *Cosmopolitan* recently.

> The moment we are married, our ghosts decide to visit and say things like, 'Well, you're married now, you need to bring home the bacon.' The answer we hear is, 'She can take care of herself.' 'I want to relax!' she will say, 'Honey, I've had a horrible day at work.' All of a sudden, we force ourselves to transform into problem-solvers and jump into action, only to find out she just wants us to listen.

At first you might think these are first-world problems, yet it's incidents like this that, gradually, over time, chip away at what men feel is expected of them. And if they don't do this in reality, they still make men feel like they do, which as we know is tantamount to the same thing.

Men aren't even allowed to be brave anymore, because as soon as they are, they are reprimanded by the press, by the police and by government for interfering in other people's lives, and for doing other people's jobs for them. If someone breaks into your house, you need to be very careful about defending yourself, because if you strike your intruder first, odds-on you'll eventually be found to have infringed their human rights.

I exaggerate, but being 'brave' is not something that we are encouraged to be or to respect anymore.

Heroism traditionally comes in many forms, and consequently has been celebrated comprehensively. There are many great quotes about bravery, including 'bravery is being the only one who knows you're afraid' (coined by the once famous but now largely forgotten American businessman Franklin P. Jones), and 'bravery is the capacity to perform properly even when scared half to death', voiced by Omar Bradley, the American general who commanded the US ground forces in the Normandy invasion of World War II. However, my favourite is the following, written by former chief of the Fire Department of New York, and one of the most famous fire fighters of all time, Edward F. Croker:

Firemen are going to get killed. When they join the department they face that fact. When a man becomes a fireman his greatest act of bravery has been accomplished. What he does after that is all in the line of work. They were not thinking of getting killed when they went where death lurked. They went there to put the fire out, and got killed. Fire fighters do not regard themselves as heroes because they do what the business requires.

But these days it's all different. These days, bravery is a word you hear every five minutes on *The X Factor*. Today, bravery is all about owning up to your inner demons, confronting your true self and thinking outside the box. Today, bravery is all about choosing fish when everyone else has ordered the lamb ('God, you're brave!'), about going blonde when all the other WAGs have dyed their hair red, about going double-breasted when most people are still going single (and very happy about it too). These days, bravery is all about admitting you actually like the records of Craig David and don't really care who knows it (yes, these days even irony is brave).

Bravery today isn't so much a character trait as a lifestyle option; it's not about judgement, but seeking attention. It's about hiring a press officer. Being brave used to be about making a decision. It still might be, although these days those decisions are very, very different.

The concept of bravery in 2016 has changed almost beyond recognition, to the point where it's been more than somewhat devalued. It seems to many to be a word, like so many others, that has been denuded of its true meaning to the extent that a *Britain's Got Talent* contestant with a sore throat is 'brave' if they decide to perform in public. These days you are brave if you're a celebrity disclosing your battered childhood to a tabloid newspaper for a vast sum of money; brave if you're a professional footballer who doesn't wear gloves when they're playing on Boxing Day; brave if you're a Hollywood leading man who decides to follow his latest worldwide blockbuster with a small, independent, black-and-white film shot on 16mm in the wilds of northern Bulgaria. A while ago, I read a piece by the political journalist Steve Richards about the then Labour government's children's education policy that was entitled – in big bold letters – 'It takes bravery to break class barriers'. Does it? No, actually, it doesn't. All it takes is someone making the right decisions, and someone else allowing that person to implement them. Bravery doesn't come into it – not by the longest piece of chalk in the world does it.

I once read a profile of the jazz guitarist Bill Frisell in the *New Yorker*, in which he was praised for his journeys into rock, pop, country, soul, 'free-form extemporisations', 'symphonic collaborations' and so on. But, of course, a career built on experimentation and curiosity can't simply be looked upon as a logical way to extend one's repertoire and experience – no, the writer praised Frisell ('Guitar Hero' screamed the headline, proudly) for being 'fearless'.

Brave? Give me one very small, wafer-thin break.

Anyone who has dipped into Antony Beevor's *Stalingrad* or Piers Brendon's *The Decline and Fall of the British Empire* will have learned a little about bravery, as, indeed, will anyone who has ever watched the seminal '70s TV series *The World at War*. Speak to a relative of anyone serving in Iraq or Afghanistan and you'll learn a little more.

Having been responsible for sending so many journalists to Iraq and Afghanistan on behalf of *GQ*, I have become used to reading their harrowing tales, not just concerning the bravery of the allied forces and the horrendous things they have been force to witness, the awful fear they have had to endure, but also the bravery of the journalists themselves. I know two *GQ* journalists – one a good friend – who have been held captive in the Middle East, and listening to them talk, hearing them tell of the constant mental torture they had to endure – not knowing if they were going to live or die from one day to the next – made me understand the real nature of bravery. I took one to lunch in London soon after he was released and every time a waiter walked behind him, he jumped. Literally jumped.

He is a properly brave man. Would he wear gloves if he played for Manchester United? Probably, but then I think he'd be forgiven.

In short, bravery, like physical strength, determination and brute force, has been diminished to such an extent that none of these attributes will ever be considered an attribute again – such is manxiety.

The wrong sex

Frankly, we feel emasculated.

'Men no longer have clearly defined roles in marriage,' says *Cosmopolitan* contributor Jon Pease.

> Our testosterone-laden brains function differently than oestrogen-created brains, and we actually crave clarity of roles to help us flourish. Women thrive on collaboration.

Men thrive on solving. I am not preaching that we go back to the Stone Age. I am suggesting that happier marriages begin with a discussion about what your women's expectations are from us.

And if those marriages break down – and these days divorces are more likely to be demanded by women – God help a father who wants proper access to his children. There is an assumption nowadays that children will live with their mother after a separation, causing divorced men who are denied custody or access to rage against a system that has penalised them for becoming what women wanted them to be in the first place.

If you trawl the problem pages of mid-market women's magazines, it is interesting to see that they are full of questions (made up or real) from women about their men, rather than themselves. Often these questions relate to their partner's inability to cope with their diminished role in a marriage or a relationship, one in which they are initially required for sex, then breeding, and then, well, what exactly?

'We know women are super competent, and don't "need" us in the traditional sense, but feeling wanted is pretty darn awesome for us, too,' says Pease.

> Not that we were taught to tell you that. The men in my
> caseload over the past six years have consistently echoed the
> desire to feel needed and important. We want to believe that
> our opinions are relevant and meaningful. Yes, we still have
> to work at it, ghosts and all, but it's a good starting point.

I have some personal experience of this myself. A few years ago, various people thought I ought to start exploring the possibility of taking up some non-executive roles, sitting on boards and advising companies on strategy and brand positioning. Two friends of mine, who spend their lives bouncing around the world rescuing companies from identity oblivion, suggested I meet some head hunters, which I duly did. Although the caveat, my friends mentioned, was almost the very first thing these head hunters told me.

Yes, that's right: I was the wrong sex.

My friends had told me that, in their considerable experience, most of the boards they sat on and most of the companies they worked on now felt under pressure to employ more women at a senior level; not for any other reason than corporate appearances. They said that the entire non-exec world had been slanted in favour of women, as many companies – particularly public companies – felt the pressure of public, media and corporate opinion to include them on their boards.

So it was when I started meeting the people whose job it is to find non-executive board members. These people – almost all of whom were women – would wait until after they had talked about my office, the journey they had just made, the coffee they had just been brought, and how things were going business-wise with myself before saying, almost apologetically, 'Well, you do realise that you're the wrong sex, don't you?'

When I said that, yes, I had heard that this was indeed the case, you could see the relief in their eyes, as though they knew they didn't have to go through the next forty-five minutes with any great sense of expectation on my part; I had a penis, and that simply wasn't good enough.

And so it proved. While I am never short of consultancy opportunities, the non-exec world has become one that has been off limits to me because of my sex.

As another friend said to me, 'So now you know what it feels like to be a woman.'

Well, maybe once upon a time, but not anymore. Because it's women who have the upper hand.

In fact, men have become so beleaguered, so unsure of themselves, that self-help books for men have started to infiltrate bookshops and large newsagents. I was in a bookshop in Marylebone the other day and there was an entire shelf of the things, instruction manuals about how to cope with our partners, our offspring, our parents, our friends, even ourselves. Obviously male identity has been so diminished, so fractured, and is now so confusing and contradictory that we need guidance in order to understand how to deal with it all. Of course, a lot of this material is incredibly helpful, such as the guidance concerning how to fix relationships with our fathers, or coming to terms with failure, disappointment or divorce. As men have a history of being able to bury problems, conflicts and psychological issues in sealable boxes, anything which encourages us to confront them can only be good. However, what most of these books are focusing on nowadays is the confused identity of men, not their ability to unlock emotions and relate to those around them.

In Steve Biddulph's *Manhood: A Guidebook for Men*, for instance, he discusses how the 'sensitive New Age guy' of the 1960s and '70s became slippery, uncommitted and narcissistic instead of caring and sharing. The fact that he was being encouraged to explore his inner life meant that at times this was all he did, often at the expense of his relationships. Women wanted men to be more sensitive and more intimate, but they didn't want them to become weaker. Biddulph argues that men need to become balanced – perfectly balanced – but he does so by encouraging us to become more fatalistic, and to develop an inner life. He says there are five truths of manhood:

1. You are going to die.

2. Life is hard.

3. You are not that important.

4. Your life is not about you.

5. You are not in control of the outcome.

However, most men aren't looking for a spiritual life, they're trying to make their way in the one they know.

Men are, predictably, their own worst enemy, as even when they're trying to make nice, they can so easily make nasty. Take this exchange from a website blog called Boycott American Women...

Tuesday 1 March 2011

NORMAL MAN REPLIES TO HATEFUL FEMINIST

HATEFUL FEMINIST says: Men are not doing what they're supposed to.

NORMAL MAN: Who are you to define what men should do? If a man defines what women do, you and the rest of the 'feminists' scream patriarchy! So why should men listen to you?

HATEFUL FEMINIST: Is it because of women spoiling them?

NORMAL MAN: Women continue to spoil the worst alpha male types, who don't appreciate it and crap on the nice guys. Who's [*sic*] fricking fault is that?

HATEFUL FEMINIST: Less men are taking the role of fathers/care takers/providers and they actually expect their spouse to continually baby them and stroke their ego even though in most cases they don't deserve such attention.

NORMAL MAN: Women don't allow men to be fathers. Your kind constantly says things like the baby is mine cause it comes out of my body. Women dump their husbands and don't allow fathers to see their kids, and the feminist-run courts allow that. If you want men to take more responsibility, you have to allow men to have ACTUAL RIGHTS. Something you and your sisters will never allow.

HATEFUL FEMINIST: In the two-parent homes I've noticed the mother playing the role as mother and father while the father is out for long periods: womanizing, betting, or doing criminal activities.

NORMAL MAN: You forgot working long hours like a slave so the princess and HER kids can have whatever they want. Typical smug modern day feminist attitude you have there.

HATEFUL FEMINIST: The wealthy tend to throw money at their problems and tend to be absent fathers due to 'work'. Has this become the average American home? The women take all the burden while the men go out and have fun. What do you think is the issue with American men?

NORMAL MAN: So if you bust your butt and provide a great life for your wife and kids then you're an evil absent male due to 'work'. If you stay home, you're a lazy bum with no ambition. BTW work is not fun and fricking games! Work, real work, important work that makes money, is hard! No one pays you a lot of money for doing nothing! If you actually had a real job, you'd understand that. And you wonder why more men don't want to sign up and marry constantly whining harpys [*sic*] such as yourself.

HATEFUL FEMINIST: What do you think is the issue with American men?

NORMAL MAN: Maybe there aren't any women worth rising to the occasion for. You're proof of that.

Part II

How did we get here?

Q: What did God say after creating man?
A: I can do so much better.

I T WASN'T AN especially auspicious occasion, yet I remember the day as though it were only yesterday. I was sitting in my ground-floor office – well, an oblong glass bunker if truth be known – in the Old Laundry, a converted workhouse in Marylebone, just a short walk from London's busiest shopping thoroughfare, Oxford Street. The Old Laundry was the HQ of *The Face* and *Arena*, where I was ensconced as a contributing editor of the former and the editor-in-chief of the latter. It was March 1991, and while it wouldn't be long before I went off to work in Fleet Street, for the time being

I was enjoying being involved in what was, at the time, one of the most influential independent publishing houses in the world – a house built by the mighty Nick Logan (the man who had previously edited the *NME* during its heyday).

It was a blazingly hot day, and I was sitting behind my desk in Armand Basi shirtsleeves, doing due diligence on a copy of *The Independent*, yet the man approaching me was wearing his usual heavy woollen overcoat. The contributors who worked for *The Face* and *Arena* were an idiosyncratic bunch, at least sartorially. The much-celebrated rock writer Nick Kent, whom we had rescued from a dwindling career at the *NME* and a methadone habit, used to come into the office wearing leather trousers with great holes in the crotch, trousers he probably hadn't taken off since 1973, when he was last on tour with the Rolling Stones. Nick was the most celebrated music critic in the world, and yet when he walked around London people thought he was about to ask for money. Then there was the stylist Ray Petri, who always strolled into the office looking like he had spent three days in front of the mirror preparing for his entrance, in his navy-blue MA-1 flying jacket, silver tab Levi's and feathered trilby. The thing is, Ray – the most sophisticated men's fashion editor of his day – was the most effortlessly cool man in the western hemisphere, and had usually thrown his clothes on as he was leaving his house.

Sean O'Hagan, while not being one of our major contributors, was known around the office for his lugubrious manner, his fondness for Stalinist indie bands, and the fact that he never appeared to take his overcoat off, even when it was sweltering outside. He had come to see me this morning to pitch an idea, one centred around a new type of male generic he had stumbled over, a new type of man, one who had out-grown the idea of the New Man, and who had turned into something called the New Lad. After listening to his somewhat rambling pitch, I told him that the idea didn't sound very plausible, and that I thought he was simply making it up.

Dismissive is how I would describe my reaction, but then I was wrong, just as I was wrong when I questioned why Tony Parsons wanted to write a piece for me a few months earlier called 'The Tattooed Jungle' – a polemic article that eventually turned into a cottage industry.

I told O'Hagan that if he really thought the thesis stood up, then he should go back to his one-bedroomed basement in Stockwell and damn well write it. Which is exactly what he did, and the piece was so convincing, and so well argued, that we published it a few weeks later ('Here Comes the New Lad').

So I have to hold my hands up and admit that it was me who was partly responsible for inflicting the New Lad on the world. For which I can only apologise. The publication in *Arena* of O'Hagan's piece set in motion a series of events that resulted in the publication of a lot of tawdry magazines that appeared to want to celebrate little but the rather more reductive and imbecilic elements of masculinity, namely the Old Lad.

As Sean explained it, the New Lad was

a rather schizoid, post-feminist fellow with an inbuilt
psychic regulator that enables him to imperceptibly alter
his consciousness according to the company he keeps.
Basically, the New Lad aspires to New Man status when
he's with women, but reverts to Old Lad type when he's
out with the boys. Clever, eh?

O'Hagan's essay identified men's sympathetic responses
to feminism, yet their inability to embrace it whole-
heartedly. As Tony Parsons would later write, in one
of the many responses to Sean's piece:

Any modern man who read Sean O'Hagan's essay had
no difficulty at all in saying – God, that's me. Sensitive,
enlightened, caring – but only up to a point, and the
point was where you had to surrender your manly soul.
Every man who read O'Hagan's treatise on the New
Lad had known nothing but girls and women who had
been shaped by decades of feminism – and so we
had been touched by it too. And we were even broadly

sympathetic to its aims, as long as we could still go to the football on a Saturday afternoon, and as long as all the stuff we really liked wasn't suddenly seen as symbolic of an oppressive patriarchal society.

O'Hagan's piece coincided with the publication of Nick Hornby's *Fever Pitch*, a book which not only elevated football to a cultural position it hadn't really held since the glory days of 1966, when England won the World Cup, but which also allowed men to wallow in their obsessional tendencies in a way that had rarely been done before, creating a publishing genre that was compounded by Hornby's next book, *High Fidelity*, which explored the male obsession with cataloguing music.

The problem was that the men in O'Hagan's piece had actually read *The Female Eunuch*, as had Hornby; but by the time the New Lad had been interpreted by the publishing industry, this new consumer appeared to be interested only in old-fashioned yobbism. Seemingly overnight, the generation of men who were coming of age in those heady days of Britpop and Britart were co-opted by a media that was intent on treating them like oafs, while celebrating all the things that magazines like *The Face* and *Arena* had tried so hard to distance themselves from.

The untuckables

To look at the dozens of men's magazines that launched in the '90s, you could have been forgiven for thinking that the Alpha Male had – perhaps unwittingly, perhaps willingly – had some sort of frontal lobotomy (and not 'a bottle in front of me'). Apparently you couldn't be a man unless everything you consumed, everything you appreciated, everything you read, watched and listened to came complete with its own inverted commas. Big yellow foam inverted commas that proved you didn't take things too seriously.

To be aspirational, to want to achieve in life, was somehow considered to be uncool. You had to read a lads' magazine and you had to drink beer straight from the bottle and you had to pretend to be a New Lad and you had to treat everything as a joke. Yuppies were considered to be too '80s, too associated with the Thatcher era, too associated with the good life. To lust after the better things in life – to learn languages, earn proper money, drive better cars and seduce more attractive, better-educated women – you had to do it ironically, as though you didn't really care. I wrote a piece about them at the time – the 'untuckables', I called them, the sort of men who wandered around with a bottle of imported Belgian beer in one hand and a copy of *Trouser Snake* in the other. They were the reductive, unacceptable face of the New Man.

Soon there was an avalanche, a veritable tsunami of magazines aimed at men who were determined not to take themselves too seriously. These were not New Lads, rather they were resolutely old-fashioned lads, men who wanted to act like boys, regardless of what age they were. First there was *Loaded*, which for eighteen months was actually tremendously funny; then a dreary old menswear magazine called *For Him Magazine* relaunched itself as the rather raunchier *FHM*; then came *Maxim, Front, Later, Eat Soup* (*Loaded* does food, which was basically a list of curry houses), *Hotdog, Bizarre, Jack, Zoo, Nuts* etc. These were colloquially known as 'lads' mags' by the media press, and for a while men couldn't get enough of them. *Loaded* had started as a terrifically smart magazine, but soon it, and all the rest, became tawdry peddlers of cheap sex, toilet humour and 'ironic' profanity. However, in truth, there was little that was ironic about any of these magazines, and when their circulations started to tumble, the only button they had to press – and press it they did, with some considerable vigour – was sex. And as we know, you only have to go down that road a little way before you start churning out pornography.

As these magazines lurched downmarket, so the internet started to be defined by pornography, making printed porn an unviable business proposition. Consequently, lads' mags started to feel a little old-fashioned, a tad embarrassing. By the end of 2015 every magazine in the sector had closed. A publishing phenomenon was no more.

What these magazines did, however, was to treat men as proper consumers, treating them the way women had been treated for generations. Rather than just buying hobby magazines, or music magazines, these magazines showed that men were legitimate targets for companies and brands selling alcohol, fashion, cars, holidays, films, books, CDs, mobile phones, sex chat lines etc. – anything, in fact. Men became objects to be marketed to, which in a way gave said men even more confidence than having magazines aimed at them. Look, they all thought to themselves, all these people want us!

Inadvertently, Sean O'Hagan had helped create not just a publishing phenomenon, but also a male advertising spree.

In reality, this had actually all been started a short while earlier, back in the '80s, with the UK launch in

1986 of *Arena*, followed by *GQ* two years later, and eventually *Esquire* in 1991. These magazines were aimed at men who wouldn't have been seen dead carrying a lads' magazine, had they existed back then. In fact, *Arena* was launched specifically at the men who bought *The Face*, as Nick Logan sensed that the time was right to launch a magazine that discerning men could call their own.

Both *Arena* and *GQ* were born on the back of a massive consumer boom, and reflected all the traditional, Route One virtues of manhood. They were born during a period when men had started to consume in ways they never had before, embracing designer lifestyles that had hitherto been denied them. Whether their readers were architects or bankers, whether they had spent their formative years reading *The Face* or *The Guardian* or the *Financial Times*, in the mid-'80s he found a place to rest his head – or, rather, a place to rest his Mont Blanc fountain pen, the keys to his Porsche 911 or the Soul II Soul CD (that place probably being a Matthew

Hilton 'Flipper' glass coffee table, complete with steel shark fins masquerading as legs).

The Best a Man Can Get

The year 1988 was the one in which *Arena* hit its stride, and also the year of *GQ*'s launch. It was the year of perestroika, the year of Harry Enfield's Thatcherite Cockney plasterer Loadsamoney, the year George Bush ('Bush forty-one') succeeded Ronald Reagan ('The Gipper'). The year 1988 saw Tom Wolfe's *The Bonfire of the Vanities* and Don DeLillo's *Libra* on every man's Tonelli Eden coffee table, saw us queuing up to see *Rain Man* and *Die Hard*, saw us careering through the city in our 325i convertibles and our Mercedes W126s listening to Neneh Cherry's 'Buffalo Stance' and *Introducing the Hardline According to Terence Trent D'Arby*, our customised in-car stereo turned all the way up to eleven and beyond. It was the year of the Lockerbie disaster, the year that Ayrton Senna won his first world championship, the year that Wimbledon famously won the FA Cup, beating the unbeatable Liverpool in the process. It was also the year that, on 27 June in Atlantic City, the undisputed world heavyweight champion Mike Tyson knocked out Michael Spinks in just ninety-one seconds. Spinks never fought again.

It was the year, lest anyone dare forget, of the yuppie – birthed into a world of opportunity, of new money, of shiny new frontiers. These magazines launched in the shadow of the City's Big Bang – London's sudden deregulation of the financial markets – born into a world where the celebration of success was no longer frowned upon. A world where aspiration was apparently an aspiration in itself. The '80s was one of the most divisive decades of the twentieth century, but when the going got tough, the tough found there were good times to be had if you just looked hard enough. Or worked hard enough. Or worked hard enough at looking hard enough. This was the world that these magazines reflected, a world full of fast cars, fast women, fast money. A world full of men who, while they understood that Gordon Gekko's 'Greed is good' credo was meant to be consumed ironically, actually rather liked the idea of it. The '80s was the decade that put the arch into post-modern architecture, the decade of the oversized car phone, the overpriced mountain bike, the overmarketed compact disc, the overstuffed Filofax, the decade of the wheel clamp, and power dressing for men (when David Bowie said that padded shoulders would become the flares of the '80s, there were few of us who doubted him, and unsurprisingly there were hardly any to be seen in the Bowie exhibition at the V&A half a generation later).

These magazines inadvertently reflected the aspirations of a generation who assumed a designer lifestyle was their birthright, a lifestyle that – for a while, at least – was defined by the matte-black dream home: by matte-black hi-fis on matte-black tech-towers in matte-black open kitchens. 'Designer' became everyone's favourite prefix – designer jeans, designer drugs, designer nightclubs (the Haçienda in Manchester, Otto Zutz in

Barcelona!), designer cars, designer lettuce. Design was everything, and everything was design.

These magazines were not just vehicles for beautiful fashion photography and esoteric/hard-hitting/amusing journalism, they also became arbiters of taste.

We were surrounded by a taste explosion, as lifestyle was suddenly becoming something of a genre in itself, almost a life choice. The prefix de jour would soon move to 'luxury' and then 'bespoke', but back then the term 'designer' was applied to everything from your matte-black TV tech tower to your snazzy Paul Smith tie.

This generation had ambition and self-fulfilment hard-wired into it from the get-go: and we liked it that way. We embraced the exercise boom as the body beautiful became a male ideal, and we all started to become educated consumers, consuming more like women in fact (the most sophisticated consumers of all). Some tried to label us New Men, but I don't think many of us were comfortable being called feminist-influenced sexual revolutionaries (not in public, anyway). In a way, both *Arena* and *GQ* were the manifestation of what we secretly knew to be true: we can have it all.

From the first issue onwards these magazines were intended as an invitation to the best party in town, a hard card of luxurious enticements. Success with style, taste and achievement, intelligence with irreverence, the ultimate urban men's tip-sheet. Top-end fun, in other words. Looking back now, one can detect a certain brittle bravado, as though we didn't really believe we were entitled to such things – but the magazines soon became successful, becoming the unironic print embodiment of the Gillette ad: The Best a Man Can Get. (Of course, our success also resulted in a generation of men for whom the height of sophistication was learning how to pronounce Gstaad correctly. Some became so good at this that they made sure to include it in every conversation they ever had, which obviously made them somewhat negligent in the entertainment department.)

Overnight, men had turned into marketing opportunities. Suddenly the advertising industry had found a way of reaching men, men who were being encouraged to update their lifestyle by dipping into fashion, by experimenting with food, by jumping on aeroplanes, upgrading their cars, and in the manner in which they approached everyone they came into contact with – be they potential spouse, potential employer or potential employee. Alpha Men became Alpha Consumers, principally because they became more feminised. He wasn't a metrosexual – I think that term was always more applicable to New York than anywhere in Britain – but he became obsessed by luxury in all its many forms.

Now we all had to watch what we wore, what we said, and how we carried ourselves.

The thing is, was it our fault, or the fault of the publishing companies? We didn't really mind being marketed to, but then is that all that we had to look forward to? Being defined by what we bought? By what we wore, and by what we said?

In the immortal words of Leiber and Stoller, 'Is that all there is?'

73

Either way, there was nothing we could do about it, and in the thirty years since the launch of *Arena* and *GQ*, we have seen the shifting tectonic movements of sexual mores, career definitions and status anxiety, a quarter of a century in which men have continued to define themselves – through ambition, through creativity, through the ever-changing prism of masculinity, and through their positions as fathers, sons, husbands and lovers.

So it's not too surprising that, having woken up and realised that we have become in many people's eyes simply consumer targets, we feel a bit cheated. A bit cheap.

But then over the years, in fact ever since the very end of World War Two, we have seen images of ourselves reflected back at us, whether we liked them or not.

One thing a man is not meant to be today is a hero. To be an old-fashioned, chivalrous male archetype who rescues the girl from the burning bridge, who punches first and asks questions later, well, he is frowned upon. Sure, Hollywood movies might be full of superheroes

– just look at the extraordinary success of the *Avengers* series – but then these films are so far removed from reality that in the public consciousness they have become CGI versions of cartoons – which is what they actually are. We love watching Robert Downey Jr as Iron Man, and we laugh at his dispassionate way with murder and his laissez-faire attitude towards human life in just the same way we would have done in a comic book; his representation on screen is almost incidental.

These days, being a hero is a fictional stereotype, not an actual one. After all, if you stand up for yourself, or protect your family from marauding villains, you'll be hauled in front of a judge and accused of tampering with someone's human rights.

I was struck by how far we have come from an appreciation of old-fashioned male values when I was reading Alex Ferguson's *Leading*, his tremendous book on football management. There is a section in the book that deals with coping with the owners of football clubs, and Ferguson describes his initial experiences at Aberdeen, the club he managed with some success before being hired to reinvent Manchester United.

'Your boss can make or break you,' he writes.

I learned that while I was at Aberdeen managing under Dick Donald. The greatest gift he gave me was unerring confidence in my capabilities. This was particularly true in my first year at the club, when we had a bumpy time. I also had to deal with the legacy of the previous manager, Billy McNeill, who had left to manage Celtic and had been popular with the players. In March 1979 I was feeling pretty despondent after Rangers beat Aberdeen 2–1 in the Scottish League Cup final. A couple of the players had made no secret of the fact that they preferred my predecessor, and the local newspaper, the *Press and Journal*, had been questioning my credentials; I said as much to Dick. He just said, 'I hired you because you can do the job. I'm not interested in what the press say. You just get on with your job. Don't moan. Be a man.'

Bear identity

The thing is, being a man these days is something we're not always allowed to be.

Just look at the way in which gay iconography has co-opted traditional, blue-collar male imagery. Take the Tom of Finland illustrations, for instance, where pneumatically muscled leather boys, bikers and lumberjacks replaced the previously stereotypical idea of gay men – namely, the effeminate sissy. These cartoons involved muscle-bound male archetypes who just happened to be gay, men in self-assertive poses who were completely in control of their surroundings. Based on Finnish mythology of lumberjacks representing strong masculinity, these images defined post-war gay men as strong, aggressive, rebellious and dominant. Not only were they sissies no more, but they had stolen the imagery of the working-class role model – something that would be compounded by the success of the Village People in a wider context in the mid-'70s. This gay fantasy band included members dressed as a policeman, a construction worker, a leather man etc. – the original recruitment ad read: 'Macho Types Wanted: Must Dance And Have A Moustache.' There was a clear sense that as well as acting as pornography, these images actually related to contemporary gay figures subverting traditional concepts of hypermasculine power in Western society. As the French sociologist Pierre Bourdieu says, the masculine, muscular body played a crucial role in working-class ideology as 'the popular valorization of physical strength as a fundamental aspect of virility and of everything that produces and supports it'.

Nowadays, when you see a man with such a clearly defined sense of identity, the inclination is to assume he's a Muscle Mary.

An extrapolation of this is 'bear identity', a gay identity that distinguishes itself from other gay identities by the physical attributes of being heavy-set and hairy, often with a beard. A big beard. The slogan of an Italian bear organisation called Orsi Italiani proudly states: 'Happy to be fat, glad to be hairy, and proud to be gay.' According to a study produced by Stanford University, the earliest known references to 'bear' as an emergent identity category among gay men came from the newsletter of the Satyrs motorcycle club in Los Angeles in 1966. According to the same report, in the early 1980s some gay men started wearing small teddy bears in their back pockets as a way of distancing themselves from the 'hanky code', the habit of wearing different types of handkerchiefs according to your sexual preference: 'The use of the teddy bear instead of bandanas was meant to rebel against the intimacy within the code and within clone culture more generally, marking an individual's desire for kissing and cuddling rather than the impersonal and emotionally detached sexual interactions typically associated with cruising for "tricks".'

The first time I went to San Francisco, in 1990, the predominantly gay Castro district was one of the places I wanted to visit as, along with Haight-Asbury, it was one of the cornerstones of 1960s US counterculture, and had become a tourist attraction as much as a hotbed of sexual insurrection. The two things that were surprising to me about the Castro were a) that it was far more aggressive than I expected it to be, and actually half a world away from the gay utopia I had been expecting; and b) there were 'bears' everywhere – big guys with long beards who all looked as though they were part of a biker gang. These men actually looked the least aggressive of anyone in the area, like roadies for a ballet troupe.

It's not just the butch iconography that has been taken from men. Just imagine for a moment the fundamental semiotics of punk. Or rather, the punk. Viewed now through the prism of recent history, we think of the punk as a glamorous if brutalist rebel, a Paul Simonon/James Dean character with perfectly peroxide hair, a designer leather jacket and sculpted cheekbones. Back in the day, the likes of Lou Reed and Jim Morrison could walk around like insects in their leather jackets and sunglasses, twitching and looking proto-cool while understanding the implicit absurdity of the 'rock-and-roll bête-noire badass pose' (in the words of crazed rock writer Lester Bangs), but now everybody can copy the emaciated, skinny-jean look – it's even in Topman and H&M. Today we tend to think of the punk ideal as rather cool, and just another link in the chain of post-WWII youth cults; the reality, however, is that the punk in his original form was something of a weed – an outcast, a skinny and probably malnourished urchin with an underdeveloped sexuality and bad skin. This version of the original punk morphed into the shoegazing archetype of the early '80s, the kind of art student who would sport a second-hand raincoat, difficult hair and a sad puppy face. This was the nerd as neurotic boy outsider, a white-trash wet weed. This stereotype still exists today in the shape of the bookish hipster, a man who has been brought up to treat women so equally that he can't distinguish them from men. This is less about gender fluidity than asexuality, where any kind of sexual definition becomes an aggressive act.

This archetype has been co-opted by the fashion industry to such an extent that he has become stereotypical. Fashion advertisements for men have often conjured up a man who bears scant relation to real life, and yet the skinny, moody, effete role model has been allowed to flourish in the fashion industry, as this is a man who many designers want to wear their clothes.

This is a nonsense, as so few of these men exist, and the ones that do probably can't afford the clothes they are being paid to model. As a magazine editor who has to commission fashion stories – something you may have reasonably expected to be a relatively easy thing to do – I have lost count of the number of times I have had to lecture the fashion editor or the photographer about the models they intend using. The creatives usually like working with new models – and are encouraged to do so by the model agencies, who are flogging fresh meat – and obviously the newer models tend to be younger than the older ones. Which means that if you're not careful you can end up with fashion stories full of beautifully luxurious, expensive designer clothes modelled by seventeen-year-olds with 26-inch waists who wouldn't be able to afford to buy them in the real world.

This is the principal conceit of the wrong kind of fashion photography: the portrayal of men as pubescent sexual objects modelling clothes in a way that pleases the designer but not the consumer.

Elsewhere, men can't even dress in a suit anymore. One might have thought that dressing in a suit was the very last bastion of male respectability, and in some respects it is. In others, however, it is social death. A few years ago, Nick Jones made a point of banning men in suits and ties from every outpost of his Soho House empire, figuring that the world had moved on to such an extent that if you were a Soho House member, you perhaps didn't want to sit next to someone at the bar who looked like your accountant (or worse, some-one who worked for your accountant).

Then of course there is the Gap Grunge issue. I first noticed this trend in the US, in 1998. I was in Oregon, writing a story on Nike, and spent my evenings wandering the streets of Portland, looking for low-level fun and trying to get the measure of the place. What I soon discovered was that, judging by the hordes of young Americans cruising the bars and the malls and the coffee shops, you didn't need a wardrobe stuffed like a trout pond to be well dressed. No, the guys in Portland didn't need a closet full of braces, cufflinks, shirt-stays, cummerbunds and regimental ties to make themselves feel tickety-boo. No, the new American uniform consisted of big, baggy check shirts, loose-fitting khaki shorts that hung down way below the knee, ironic baseball caps, heavily bolstered walking boots and goatee beards.

Gap Grunge, I called it, and it was soon to take over the world.

Walk through the downtown area of any large American town today and you'll see thousands of men still dressed this way, while the only men wearing suits will be those unlucky souls working in the service industry, behind the desk in a hotel, say, or in a mobile phone shop or a stationer's.

And now it's over here – big time, as Ricky Gervais's David Brent might once have said. But while Gap have now moved into a more fashion-conscious arena (more upmarket, less, er, beige), this modern civilian army is now far more likely to be dressed by Abercrombie & Fitch, the American leisure company (whose marketing ploy appears still to involve employing near-naked models as sales assistants).

This look has become the new orthodoxy; as American as cherry pie, chewing gum and fast food. No matter that this suburban army may revel in the delights of alternative rock and nose rings, no matter that they might like to think of themselves as hip, they are as normal as normal can be – making anyone who wears a suit seem positively reactionary.

Take a look around and you'll see that once more Britain has become a victim of American imperialism, as we all exchange our French cuffs and polished brogues for clothes that have the capacity to make anyone wearing them look like a sexed-up lumberjack working for an internet start-up. Walking around Hampstead one Sunday last year, as the streets filled with young families, every man under the age of fifty appeared to be wearing a pair of baggy khaki shorts; it was as if the council had decided to stage an impromptu street party based on *It Ain't Half Hot Mum*. Although they were all wearing headphones instead of pith helmets. Whatever happened to our famous Dunkirk spirit? What in God's name happened to our infamous eccentricity and dogged individualism?

The Brits even started wearing this uniform abroad, where the ensemble has taken on a different hue. A while ago I found myself in a horrible mock-Tudor pub in Santa Monica, the only place in Los Angeles that appeared to be showing a particular Champions League game. It was so completely out of character with the rest of the area's pastel Modernist buildings that I immediately christened the style Chav Tudor. But it did have a TV.

Having paid $10 each for the privilege of standing in a dingy, smelly bar that would have been considered too low-rent for the Old Kent Road, we found ourselves surrounded by eighty to a hundred Ronnie Biggs looka-likes. And every one of them seemed to be a Cockney. We knew this because they all found it impossible to say anything without including the well-worn phrase 'Goo-on-my-son'. For example: 'Sheila, any danger of another plate of chicken wings goo-on-my-son?', or 'Goo-on-my-son can I pinch one of your fags?'

But it wasn't the fact that they were from London that intrigued us, it was the fact that all of them looked between the ages of forty-five and sixty, and were wearing earrings, baggy polo shirts, humungous khaki shorts with big utility belts and large, dusty work boots. That's right, they all looked like clones. Every man jack of them looked as if he'd just stepped out of a Tom of Finland cartoon. Either that, or he'd stepped out of the queue to get into Heaven, the nightclub that was the hippest gay venue in London during the '80s.

Even the ones wearing football shirts looked like Big Butch Marys.

Here was a uniform that seemingly united everyone: straights, gays, Americans, Cockneys, suburbanites, alt-rockers – the whole shooting match. These days, Gap Grunge is as ubiquitous as ubiquity itself. But maybe I shouldn't be so down on it, maybe I shouldn't be quite so churlish. Maybe I'm wrong, and maybe it's true that beauty really is in the eye of the beholder. Recognising Pablo Picasso in a train compartment, a man inquired of the artist why he did not paint people 'the way they really are'. Scowling a little, Picasso asked what he meant by that expression. And so the man opened his wallet and took out a photograph of his beloved wife, saying, 'That's my wife.'

Picasso stared at the snapshot for a while before saying, quietly, 'Isn't she rather small and flat?'

The late actor-turned-writer Colin Welland (who would go on to write the screenplay for *Chariots of Fire*) had it about right. The star of *Roll On Four O'Clock*,

Welland's early-'60s TV play about the staff and pupils of a Manchester secondary modern, was a teenage outcast called 'Pansy' Peter Latimer. Wearing blue jeans, a fawn roll-neck sweater, a blond fop fringe and a black leather jacket with 'Pete' written on the back in round silver studs, Latimer was the school oddball – tormented, bullied and relentlessly beaten up.

'Latimer, he's a special case,' says one teacher. 'He's not a bad lad,' says another, 'for a creep.'

Latimer was Britain's first home-grown Neurotic Boy Outsider who wasn't a singer or an actor. He was a bona fide internalised rebel; a teacher's pet who hates games, an outsider who longs for acceptance. It's not difficult to see where Morrissey drew his inspiration from, and it's surprising that 'Pansy' Pete hasn't turned up on the cover of one of Morrissey's records, a northern role model to rival Pat Phoenix in *Coronation Street* or Albert Finney in *Saturday Night and Sunday Morning*.

There are few more classic pop archetypes than the Neurotic Boy Outsider. Continually wrestling with those damn inner demons, the NBO displays an obvious nervousness, often disguised with a hint of sexual ambiguity. He traditionally wears a frown and a leather jacket, tries to look like James Dean, Morrissey or Kurt Cobain, conducts interviews in a mordant manner, and always looks concerned.

In pop promos he will be seen hitching along a lonely desert road, moody and alone (NBOs are always unaccompanied), gazing skyward, in search of divine intervention, or perhaps a new pair of sunglasses. He is, above all else, determinedly aloof, if not a little evangelical (NBOs are never far from displaying an unhealthy Messiah complex).

And for several years now there has been a new pop archetype, 'the Woodsman', the bearded loner in the lumberjack shirt with a scowl, a singer of indeterminate age who fronts a band of sullen subordinates who can't quite believe how successful they are. Woodsmen are everywhere. The big one is Bon Iver's Justin Vernon, followed in no particular order by The Decemberists,

Fleet Foxes, Arcade Fire, Great Lake Swimmers, Band of Horses, Volcano Choir, Iron & Wine, My Morning Jacket and all the rest. When the *New Yorker* published a piece about My Morning Jacket a while ago, they said, 'You know these guys are bearded without seeing a photograph of them.'

Essentially they look like hipsters, only without the fine Savile Row threads.

There is a snake-like litany of Woodsmen in pop, all the way from Neil Young to Calexico, yet there have never been so many of them as there are today, never been so many pop groups who talk wistfully of remote cabins in northwest Wisconsin or renovated chicken shacks in the Californian woods, rather than infamous Hollywood groupies, and whose lyrics focus so much on isolation and displacement. There are no smiles, only faraway looks and Fleet Foxes fashion. As *GQ*'s Jamie Millar said not so long ago, 'Think lumberjack checks, waxed jackets and just generally looking as heritage as they sound.' The music is often wispy, acoustic and decidedly lo-fi, music to look forward to a long hard winter to. Many find this sort of thing uplifting – 'Listening to Bon Iver's *Bon Iver* is an activity comparable to lying in the grass of a vast garden replete with brightly colored flowers,' wrote one critic. 'Patches of crimson, and marigold, and periwinkle, and violet, and peach on grassy beds, verdant and luscious with dew.' And yet the enjoyment has to be solitary: 'On a gently sunny day, with a cloud or two drifting by, and you are alone to observe this.'

Given the success of modern folk in Britain – Noah and the Whale, Laura Marling, King Charles, elements of Ed Sheeran – you might think there are Woodsmen here too, and yet we are too parochial to have spawned any convincing examples; our countryside is too manicured, and at Mumford & Sons gigs they tell jokes between songs. Which, I suppose, is why we have the hipster instead.

Thankfully, the Woodsman doesn't appear quite so desperate as the Neurotic Boy Outsider to tell everyone how unhappy he is, preferring to stare mournfully out at the world from publicity pictures and CD covers. NBOs always have to generate attention, and as they are nothing if not show-offs, always have to go public about being private. I remember a classic example of this. It was 1984, in the Soho Brasserie in London's Old Compton Street. There he was, this lanky NBO, a throwback to the '70s – all gaunt and second-hand – sitting by himself, surrounded on other tables by braying '80s would-be whiz-kids – colourful young things with gaudy clothes and short attention spans talking about money, magazines, travel and nightclubs. The NBO was a reading a Penguin Modern Classic.

As I passed him on my way out, I noticed that the book was upside down.

Even so, like many men of his generation, my NBO had bought into his own little dream, one that bore scant relation to reality. Uninterested in the identity options available to him, he had resorted to dressing up. But I was damned if I was going to feel sorry for him.

Part Three

Part III

What and
where next?

'Men are from Earth, women are from Earth.
Deal with it.'

— GEORGE CARLIN

The decline of men

I F YOU WERE mad enough to read Guy Garcia's 2008 book *The Decline of Men: How the American Male is Tuning Out, Giving Up, and Flipping Off His Future*, you would have entered a world where the male of the species is being out-gunned, out-flanked and out-shone by women, a world where men have been struggling to redefine what it actually means to be a man today. And that's meant to be me. And maybe you (if you are a man, that is).

In a detailed exploration of contemporary American manhood, *The Decline of Men* attempted to show how the male sex is ultimately doomed. According to Garcia, our confusion has led to rampant male malaise, which has left many of us feeling alienated and disconnected. Unable to communicate our frustrated thoughts or emotions effectively, too many of us are apparently slacking off and opting out of our manly obligations, producing an entire generation of men who are failing to live up to our potential while failing the mothers, wives and girlfriends who love us.

The Decline of Men was sold as a wake-up call to this distressing state of affairs. Believe Garcia and you'd believe that, rather than working hard to achieve top grades or a promotion at work, too many men – and he was really talking about the North American male here – squander their energy tracking their fantasy football league scores or mastering the latest video game. Men drop out of school at a far higher rate than women and are far likelier to die early because of poor health habits. Even the male Y chromosome is said to be at risk of disappearing altogether one day. The author attempted to show how the feminist movement empowered women but in essence castrated an entire nation of men. And believe the hype and you'd believe that *The Decline of Men* shed light on a problem that has wreaked havoc on the family, urging men and women to look past the gender wars to address this national emergency together.

His thesis revolved – and indeed still revolves – around the spurious 'fact' that men are becoming more reductive – more stupid, less ambitious and so feminised that they are starting to be subordinate to their female counterparts. According to the author, we are being emasculated by women, unable to cope with the onslaught of a female-dominated society.

Haven't you heard all this before?

Using figures which feel as though they have been conjured from a laptop calculator almost at will, we're told that women can't find suitable men, and that we are all sitting around scratching our front bottoms, drinking far too much imported beer and watching daytime TV.

However, when Garcia says, 'The crisis facing males in America is nothing less than a national emergency with economic, sociological, and cultural ramifications for both men and women, and for generations to come,' he is simply talking the talk and singing the song of someone trying to sell a book.

His thesis involves genetics (women have always been better at processing information), society (women are now as fully emancipated as men) and positive discrimination (women are getting the good jobs, while us men sit around at home playing computer games). He asserts – and maybe there are many women out there who want to believe him – that men are starting to feel skittish and out of sorts in an increasingly ambisexual world, with their very sense of manhood imploding. This is bolstered by surveys and studies that feel as though they have been carefully plucked from the YouGov tree, and used in evidence against us. At one point he cites a study of 1,500 men in Massachusetts, reported in the *Journal of Clinical Endocrinology and Metabolism* in 2007, that found a population-wide decline in men's testosterone levels over the past twenty years. In a commentary accompanying the report, Shalender Bhasin, a doctor at Boston Medical Center, said that it would be unwise to dismiss the findings 'as mere statistical aberrations because of the potential threat these trends – if confirmed – pose to the survival of the human race and other living residents of our planet'.

However, if you look at the small print, you see that the testosterone levels allegedly dropped by only 1.2 per cent per year. And frankly, my friend, I still get angry, thank you very much, and one of the things I can easily get angry about is silly books like this.

The thing is, Garcia's argument is not a new one, and there has been talk of the feminisation of men for at least the last twenty-five years. Over a decade ago, Harvey Mansfield, the then professor of politics at Harvard, in a paper called 'Is Manliness a Virtue?', pondered the strange way in which American political correctness had all but eliminated the possibility of considering any male trait valuable. His point was that masculinity alone may well be destructive but, allied to reason, it becomes creative. In other words, he said, 'The best that we are springs from the operation of reason driven by a complementarity of sexually determined traits.' As we said in *GQ* when this paper was published, 'It should hardly need saying, but we cannot do without each other.'

And while it is certainly true that more girls than ever before are now taking higher and further education (and speaking as the father of two teenage girls I'm deliriously happy about this), this is the natural consequence of the generational acceptance of young women's continued emancipation. It does not mean, as Garcia suggests, that us men are wandering the hostile savannahs of the twenty-first century, hounded by gene-counting scientists and assailed by blunt words and well-honed arguments, feeling so intimidated that we no longer want to study in great numbers.

In America, where the book was first published, the reaction to Garcia's interpretations was lukewarm, to say the least. Take this from the *Boston Globe*:

> Garcia does make some valid points, especially when he resorts to real data and nuanced analysis. His discussions of the growing education gender gap and the negative effect of absent fathers on masculine identity are thoughtful and persuasive. But each subtle moment is tempered by another head-spinning girl-hating move, like a lecture on evolutionary theory from the heretofore-unheralded scientific authority Richard Parsons, chief executive of Time Warner ('Almost from the beginning of man's time on earth,' Parsons proclaims, 'his role has been as the protector-provider') or Ken's interior monologue (yes, that Ken) after Barbie tosses him 'aside like last year's Prada handbag'.

Garcia's book does indeed repeat some interesting points, specifically that the erosion of traditional working-class jobs for men has created a tension that has led to an emerging underclass – particularly for young black men – as well as the fact that women are approaching parity in the workplace. And although Garcia's book is based largely on research carried out in the United States, there are echoes of the positive discrimination he mentions over here. A few years ago, the Labour government, in their finite wisdom, decided to float some new discriminatory policies concerning employment law. One of the by-products of having spent a considerable amount of my life working for newspapers is that towards the end of March I begin looking forward to reading April Fools stories in the dailies. I thought I'd found one when I read that Labour ministers were preparing a law that would allow bosses to give priority for jobs and promotion to women and non-Caucasian applicants. Under a change in discrimination law then being drawn up by Equalities Minister Harriet Harman, white men could be legally blocked from being promoted, and employers would be allowed to give jobs to qualified minority candidates in preference to other candidates. Which potentially meant me. So, having made the gargantuan error of voting for a Labour government in 1997, my reward was being discriminated against because I was not a different colour. And because I was not a woman. The Labour Party called this 'positive action' or 'positive discrimination', although from where I was looking it simply seemed like social engineering.

Naturally, none of this nonsense came to pass.

Guy Garcia's worldview is a spurious one, and reminds me somewhat of Niagara Falls, and in particular in the way in which people call it the most amazing sight in the world. If you look at Niagara Falls, it is certainly impressively beautiful, but if you move your head only five millimetres in either direction you will see the detritus of tacky Canadian/American commercialism, with cheap hotels and gift shops cluttering up your view. Because Niagara Falls is surrounded by rubbish.

The author also finds a few men who are not swimming against the tide, and who are perfectly happy being emasculated. 'Women are playing a bigger role, but I think it's a good thing,' said one affable, 34-year-old software designer in the Washington, D.C. area, who said he had no problem working for a woman (but who obviously didn't want his name used in Garcia's book). 'Change is difficult, though, and some guys will have an identity crisis.' But then Garcia kicks in again with one of his ludicrous calls to arms: 'To put it in bluntly male terms, those who fail to adapt may find their next position is at the end of an unemployment line.'

There were also some shockingly banal lines in his book: 'Men are notoriously self-destructive. They smoke more than women. They drink more than women. They are prone to risky behaviour, don't like to admit they are feeling pain, and avoid visits to the doctor.' Get away! We also like fast cars, sport, sexy girls in short skirts and the occasionally misogynist prose of Philip Roth, Martin Amis and Jeremy Clarkson. And we like it that way.

In 2008, it was already a book that was woefully out of date, a book appealing to the sort of man who once read *Loaded* and *Maxim* and who perhaps felt unable to cope in a world where the New Lad was shunned. But why on earth did they buy into this world in the first place?

Guy Garcia was wrong, and quite fundamentally so. Men have never had it so good. We have embraced feminism as much as we are prepared to, we have managed to convince our wives and girlfriends that going to lap-dancing clubs is socially respectable, and there are now as many manbags on the high street as there are handbags. We can shop like women, behave like women, and still find time to go down the pub and be men. We have magazines, but we still have newspapers. Cars are designed to be chosen by women, but are still driven by men. We are still breadwinners, but so are our partners, making it easier for us to offset the mortgage. We get paternity leave but thankfully we still don't have to give birth (not unless we want to, of course). We can still take women out on dates, although often it's the women who like to pick up the bill. And because women feel so emancipated, they often want to have sex on the first date (and often initiate it). And, to paraphrase a *GQ* alumnus, while we might still argue about who takes out the rubbish, at least we have better skin these days.

Also, in a climate where all anyone can talk about is gender fluidity, isn't all this talk of the sex wars terribly old-fashioned? Sure, I worry that teenage boys are having their minds warped by exponential amounts of free, digital, hardcore pornography, but I feel much worse for the teenage girls who are all now expected to behave like grateful porn stars.

Honestly, at the time I thought Guy Garcia was nothing but a pussy-whipped fool. But there is an increasingly loud chorus out there full of men who are starting to worry about how the world has changed. And it's not because of female emancipation, it's because of male emancipation.

And they don't like it.

Frankly, I've always felt that manxiety was simply an

overreaction to a welcome redressing of the balance of the sexes. A lot of this bleating from men I found farcical, to be honest, and no more farcical than the results of a survey conducted for Jacamo menswear. Of course, we all know that manxiety can often be expressed through an insecurity about the way we look. In this particular survey, which focused on the way in which men feel inadequate (just when did men become the most analysed consumers in the country?), the results made my heart sink. The nationwide survey of 2,500 men revealed almost half (48 per cent) desperately want to lose weight and two in five (41 per cent) want to tone up, while 54 per cent are most unhappy with their midriff. Apparently, one complaint shared by those suffering with manxiety is watching films or television programmes that constantly feature unrealistically attractive men with good bodies. Around one in sixteen say this is made worse when their partner looks at images of men with fantastic bodies they don't feel they could ever achieve.

Ah, bless them.

Jenni Bamford, the spokeswoman for Jacamo menswear, said:

> The idea of having a 'perfect' body is an unrealistic and unobtainable ideal that can have long-lasting consequences for people's mental and physical wellbeing. We hope 'The Modern Man-ual' gives men the chance to talk about their concerns about body image along with encouraging a conversation around how retailers, advertisers and the media portray men to better reflect the diversity of the healthy male population. With more than twenty-four million men in Britain, it can only help to normalise this topic with both men and those influential in his life.

Seriously? According to the survey, these are the top ten causes of physical manxiety:

1) Having to uncover on a beach when surrounded by other fit men – 20 per cent.

2) Being teased by friends about my appearance – 19 per cent.

3) Watching films or television programmes starring attractive men with good bodies – 16 per cent.

4) Seeing pictures of men in advertising and media with bodies they feel they will never be able to achieve – 16 per cent.

5) Being in a changing room with younger or more attractive men – 14 per cent.

6) My friends having good bodies – 13 per cent.

7) My partner looking at images of men with bodies I feel I could never achieve – 7 per cent.

8) Being compared to my partner's ex-partners – 4 per cent.

9) My partner having a really good body – 4 per cent.

10) Being compared to my siblings – 3 per cent.

Now, I'm not sure what's to be done about the findings of this particular survey, because if we take them at face value then it seems that thirty years of intense consumer activity has just produced a generation of emotionally stunted, insecure men who appear to be intimidated by any representation of virtuoso male physicality. Honestly, would you trust a man who says that he is intimidated by his wife's beauty?

Anyway, I think this current so-called desperation among men might just be a generational thing. The millennial men I know don't seem to carry the same baggage or have the same hang-ups as their elder brothers, older friends or fathers. The millennials I know have as many female friends as male friends, they don't appear to be hidebound by tradition, and certainly don't worry about anything approaching conformity. They tend to have a far more laissez-faire attitude towards their careers, and appear to be far less concerned about owning property, or pursuing the more traditional signifiers of success. In fact, they don't seem to worry about much, apart from their ability to enjoy themselves on their own terms. The insecurities they have seem to be far less existential, while the idea that peer pressure plays any undue part in their lives seems almost farcical. In some respects, millennial men appear to be much less macho than their predecessors, far less concerned with concepts of maleness. Which is one of the reasons you rarely see groups of same-sex millennials; to them, everyone really *is* equal. Which means that feminism has actually had a much greater effect than some feminists think. Millennials usually possess vast amounts of confidence and tolerance, but also tend to be rather narcissistic. What they very much aren't is judgemental, and I've yet to meet one (a millennial man, that is) who wouldn't consider himself a feminist. They are civic-minded, pathologically concerned about the environment, and touchy about race. I was watching a clip of 'China Girl' on the news when David Bowie died, and one of the younger members of staff said, 'Can he say that? "China Girl", I mean. Isn't it a bit, you know…?' And as for 'Girl', well that was pejorative in the extreme.

As for those men who aren't millennials, those men who still worry about being men, well, enough is enough. Seriously, what is your problem? Do you *really* want to join a support group?

Of course, there have been men's movements before. Twenty-five years ago the organisation that was all the rage was Robert Bly's mythopoetic men's movement, an idea that started as a reaction to the second wave of feminism, and which aimed to 'liberate' men from what Bly called the constraints of the modern world, which kept them from 'being in touch with their true masculine nature'. According to Bly, men had become unduly feminised by the modern urban experience, while the movement sought to restore the 'deep masculine' to men who have lost it because of their lifestyle.

Seriously, this was a big deal at the time. These mythopoetic men performed shamanistic rituals at their gatherings, which according to Bly were meant to imitate those performed by tribal societies when men initiated boys into a deeply essential, natural manhood. If you were a boy, you learned from your elders, preferably without a shirt, in the woods.

We don't need a men's movement; we don't need Robert Bly. What we need is common sense, or what the photographer David Bailey calls uncommon sense – 'Because there appears to be so little of it' – and a little more understanding of how the sex wars have changed over recent years. In a nutshell, men are complaining about being consumer targets, complaining about becoming invisible both in the workplace and at home, complaining about becoming stereotyped in the media, and complaining about being perceived as vulnerable and – yes, it's finally come to this – the weaker sex. To which I am forced to say: grow a pair. Men who complain about these contravening issues are simply experiencing what women have had to deal with for centuries, being subjected to a series of randomly orchestrated rules and regulations that ultimately undermine them. Put bluntly, we wanted the permission to wear red leather trousers and, now we've got it, no one is taking us seriously.

So I'm not too sure that we need a new men's movement, or indeed another colour-by-number manifesto. We simply need to stop complaining about our lot in life, to stop wallowing in manxiety. You don't need to act like a Neanderthal to get on in the world, and nor do you need to act like a milksop.

Let's face it, it's great to be a man. So man up, bitch.